Amaury Teillard

Principles of liability in European environmental law

Amaury Teillard

Principles of liability in European environmental law

Comparison with the United States

ScienciaScripts

Imprint

Any brand names and product names mentioned in this book are subject to trademark, brand or patent protection and are trademarks or registered trademarks of their respective holders. The use of brand names, product names, common names, trade names, product descriptions etc. even without a particular marking in this work is in no way to be construed to mean that such names may be regarded as unrestricted in respect of trademark and brand protection legislation and could thus be used by anyone.

Cover image: www.ingimage.com

This book is a translation from the original published under ISBN 978-620-2-28214-7.

Publisher:
Sciencia Scripts
is a trademark of
Dodo Books Indian Ocean Ltd. and OmniScriptum S.R.L publishing group

120 High Road, East Finchley, London, N2 9ED, United Kingdom
Str. Armeneasca 28/1, office 1, Chisinau MD-2012, Republic of Moldova, Europe
Printed at: see last page
ISBN: 978-620-5-88722-6

Contents

Introduction 2

TITLE 1 : Environmental protection through the application of the polluter-pays principle. 6

Chapter 1: The Polluter Pays Principle applied in the United States by the C.E.R.C.L.A. Act7

Chapter 2: The liability regime envisaged by the Europeans 13

Second Title : The recent evolution of the European liability regime for environmental damage 32

Chapter 1: The principles developed in European law by the 2004 directive 33

Chapter 2: Possible improvements 43

BIBLIOGRAPHY 51

Introduction

Environmental law is a hot topic in all Western countries. Or rather all industrialized countries that have the financial means to deal with the material consequences of environmental damage.

Today the natural state in which we live seems deeply destabilized by human action: environmental alerts are frequently launched, reminders of former disasters, such as that of Chernobyl in April 1986 are regularly asserted[1] .

Originally, environmental damage was seen as a necessary consequence of industrial progress.

This perception of things began to evolve towards the end of the 1950s, with two major phenomena that marked society. At that time, the prospect of using nuclear energy for civil purposes made lawyers think about setting up compensation systems. In addition, the oil spills[2] left their mark on people's minds, accelerating the process of reflection on a liability regime for environmental damage.

The first French law on water was voted in 1964. But some authors situate the birth of environmental law in La Roche sur Yon in 1976[3] . It was there that the Minister of Justice made this declaration: "(...) the recognition of a right to the quality of life is emerging as an essential requirement of our society. By its vital, inalienable and imprescriptible character, this right is similar to the fundamental rights of the person"[4] .

The international community began to take an interest in the environment at about the same time. Unesco, in September 1989 in Vancouver (Canada), declared "The survival of the planet is now a major and immediate concern. The present situation demands that urgent measures be taken (...). There is not much time left: any delay in establishing a global eco-cultural peace will only increase the cost of survival. These are very alarmist words.

This has had an impact on liability regimes for environmental damage. States have adopted a plethora of texts[5] , severe towards polluters[6] .

---

1 Patricia Savin, Le droit à l'environnement, Gaz. Pal. Vend.17, Sat.18 March 2006, p. 52.
2 Torrey-Canyon in 1967, Amoco-Cadiz in 1978, Exxon Valdez in 1985.
3 Michel Prieur, L'environnement entre dans la Constitution, LPA, n° 134, 7 July 2005, p.14.
4 Revue Juridique de l'environnement, 1976, n° 3-4, p.13.
5 Paris Convention of 29 July 1960 on nuclear energy; Vienna Convention of 21 May 1963 on nuclear damage; Brussels Convention of 1962 on nuclear ship operators; Washington Convention of 1972 on space objects; Another Brussels Convention on oil pollution in 1969; Geneva Convention of 13 November 1979 on

The European Community has also sought to protect its environment. First of all, it has protected it as an essential part of the economy, since any attack on this environment destabilizes the economic relations between Member States.

It is only recently that it has admitted the responsibility of polluters, without any reference to the economy.

European environmental liability law is therefore in the process of being formed, with a proliferation of texts[7] .

One of the essential questions is to understand what exactly the concept of environmental damage in Community law refers to.

The Petit Robert gives us a definition of the environment: "All the natural (physical, chemical, biological) and cultural (sociological) conditions likely to affect living organisms and human activities.

It is therefore, in a broad sense, everything that surrounds man, in general.

It is also sometimes said that the environment is the "set of natural (physical, chemical, biological) and cultural (sociological) conditions in which living organisms (in particular man) develop. The environment can be subdivided into well-characterized and distinct environments: interior environment, culture environment, uterine environment, ... ".[8]

A legal definition can be found in the ISO 14001/1996 standard: the environment is "the environment in which an organism functions, including air, land, natural resources, flora, fauna, human beings, and their interrelationships".

All these definitions include the man in the environment since it is understood in a very broad sense (it can be uterine, cultural).

In fact, the whole question is to know if the man is put in opposition to the environment, or if he is part of it.

Another definition draws our attention: for the geographer Pierre George, the environment is the "set of elements which, in the complexity of their relations, constitute the framework,

---

long-range atmospheric pollution; Basel Convention of 22 March 1989 on the disposal and transport of hazardous materials. Source: Jurisclasseur International, Civil Liability p. 19s.

6 Christian Larroumet, La responsabilité civile en matière d'environnement, Le projet de Convention du Conseil de l'Europe et le Livre vert de la Commission des Communautés européennes, Dalloz 1994, chron. p. 101.

7 In 2004, there were 230 European texts on the environment, including 130 directives. Source: Andrée Brunet, La régulation juridique des questions environnementales et le principe de subsidiarité, Gaz. Pal. Vend. 11, Sam. 12 June 2004, p. 1705.

8 Website: psychobiology.ouvaton.org/glossary/txt-p06.20-04-glossary.htm

the environment, the conditions of life for the man." (1970)[9] .

This definition emphasizes the links between the components of the environment (atmosphere, lithosphere, biosphere and hydrosphere) and human societies. Surprisingly enough, it is this definition, and not the more legal one of the ISO 14001-1996 standard, which seems to be the closest to the European Union's idea of the environment. Indeed, it contrasts the environment and the people who live in it, and therefore contrasts the damage caused to people and the damage caused to the environment.

This has major consequences for the acceptance of reparable damage under the environmental liability regime. But the content of the environment is difficult to grasp.

Until now, Community texts have focused on specific concepts, such as water, waste and the biosphere, but have never given a general definition of the environment. This is one of the points that the new Community environmental liability law will try to resolve.

What is certain is that the environment appears today as an element of the common heritage that each generation receives from the preceding ones and must preserve, in turn, in order to transmit it to the following generations. From this point of view, environmental law can no longer be understood as the guarantee of the property of a single individual, but rather of an entire community[10] . It is no longer linked to the idea of property, it exists by itself, and this is one of the great innovations of modern European Union law.

As Michel Prieur has said, "the appearance of a new branch of law, while it does not necessarily imply the existence of a separate jurisdiction, can be accepted from the moment when a certain particularism appears around a new object.[11] This particularism of European environmental law in the field of liability is today indisputable. The confrontation of the constituent elements of liability with the particularity of ecological damage necessarily calls for original solutions.

The question is which principle of responsibility the European Union has sought to

---

9 Website: http://eduscol.education.fr/D0185/concepts.htm
10 Duguit and some other authors, from the end of the 19th century onwards, were inspired by biology to draw conclusions about the place of man in biodiversity, and the consequences that he should draw from it as regards his actions. By this observation, they will support that the man is a component of the society in which he lives, as a cell can be of the organism to which it belongs: dependent on the others, each one should, according to this analysis, act in the collective interest, at the same time of his fellow men, and of the future generations. It is from this period that was born the idea that the environment is an element of the common heritage, and that then developed that of its defense in a solidarist way. Cf. Jérôme Attard, Contrats et environnement : quand l'obligation d'information devient instrument de développement durable, LPA, 26 January 2006, n°19, p.7.
11 Michel Prieur, "Droit de l'environnement", Précis Dalloz, 4th edition, p.9.

respect in order to best defend the interests of the environment.

The polluter-pays principle had international application, and it was therefore natural that the European Union turned to it as the basis for its future liability regime for environmental damage.

The polluter-pays principle initially had a financial rather than a legal dimension. But the primary concern of States, under pressure from public opinion, was to see the damage caused to the environment repaired[12] ; the principle seemed to be the most appropriate.

The essential guidelines of European law were set out in the "Green Paper" on the repair of environmental damage presented by the European Parliament's Committee on 14 May 1993.

But the drawbacks of such a system soon became apparent. It became clear that the polluter-pays principle is legally impossible to apply. Other legal regimes have already attempted to apply it to environmental liability.

Thus, the United States had sought to apply this principle to corporate liability. But this proved to be very dangerous legally and financially. This is the same conclusion that the European Commission came to after the publication of the 1993 Green Paper.

Today, the European Union is abandoning the polluter-pays principle and turning to the fault-based liability system. Thus, the directive of April 21, 2004, which aims to create a general system of liability for damage caused to the environment, integrates the notion of fault. However, parallel developments in European law on the subject are to be observed, in particular with regard to the use of the contractual relations of the possible polluters in the calling into question of the liability.

We shall therefore first see how the various legal systems have attempted to apply the polluter-pays principle, and the flaws that led to its abandonment (I), before looking at the current development of environmental liability in European law (II).

---

12 Geneviève Viney, Les principaux aspects de la responsabilité civile des entreprises pour atteinte à l'environnement en droit français, JCP 1996, I.3900.

TITLE 1 : Environmental protection through the application of the polluter-pays principle

This principle remained for a long time the absolute principle in the protection of the environment in the EEC and then in the European Union.

However, this principle was not born in Europe; it was first applied in the United States, which had made it a principle of absolute responsibility in case of damage to the environment. This very principle was twisted by American law, finally detaching the payer from the polluter.

Many authors[13] consider it essential to understand the US environmental liability regime before beginning to study how the principle has been implemented in European law.

The study of the American liability regime shows that it closely resembles the regime set out in the European Union's Green Paper. Therefore, to study it (Chapter 1) is to study the consequences that a liability regime based on the polluter-pays principle could have in the European Union (Chapter 2).

---

13 See in particular Vincent Sol, Un droit en pleine évolution, LPA 8 août 2000, n°157, p.18; from the same author, Sanctions et responsabilité en droit de l'environnement : l'expérience américaine, Revue de droit des affaires internationales, n°7, 1993, p.869 Patrick Thieffry, l'opportunité d'une responsabilité communautaire du pollueur ; les distorsions entre les Etats membres et les enseignements de l'expérience américaine, RIDC, 1-1994, p.103s. and his conclusion p.123 : " l'expérience américaine doit absolument être prise en compte ".

Chapter 1: The Polluter Pays Principle applied in the United States by the C.E.R.C.L.A. Act

The United States, urged to intervene in the face of the pollution of environmental sites (section 1), adopted a liability regime based on the polluter-pays principle (section 2), a regime that is open to criticism because of its negative effects on the economy and the law (section 3).

Section 1 : The motivations of this law

Like Europe in the 1970s, the United States found itself with an inordinate number of polluted sites in a short period of time. It was often difficult, if not impossible, to find those responsible, due to the lack of a legal regime adapted to this search. The State was almost forced to remediate at its own expense, at least for the most urgent and dangerous sites.

The case that led the U.S. government to react is the *Love Central* case. In this case, 20,000 tons of toxic products were discovered buried in a river bed, forcing the State to order the evacuation of all the neighboring houses. Faced with the urgency of the situation, Congress introduced a law, which was quickly adopted, allowing companies to be responsible for the rehabilitation of polluted sites - estimated at 35,000 at the time[14] - by means of a simplified liability regime.

Section 2 : The legal system put in place

The regime for protecting the environment through corporate liability is made up of several statutes, but the main one is the *Comprehensive Environmental Response Compensation and Liability Act (CERCLA),* more commonly known as the "Superfund Act" of 1980.

This superfund is financed by all polluting parties, in a joint and several manner, to reimburse the *Environmental Protection Agency* for the costs of restoring the environment and repairing damage to natural resources. The law allows for the identification of what it calls "potentially polluting parties. In the mid-1990s, the fund was $1.7 billion.

The system it establishes is rather original in terms of the liability of operators and owners and the causal link. These two points are understood in a very broad manner by the law.

---

14 Vincent Sol, Sanctions et responsabilité en droit de l'environnement : l'expérience américaine, Revue des affaires internationales, n°7, 1993, p.869.

§1 What a pity taken into account

The damages taken into account are all damages of any kind to the environment and natural resources caused by the activity of a site emitting hazardous substances.

§2 Which managers

The system was primarily designed to find payers, rather than responsible parties. The law has therefore broadened the acceptance of those responsible for a site, and in so doing has called into question the very idea of the polluter paying. The C.E.R.C.L.A. law includes as responsible the "owners and operators of a site" that caused the pollution resulting from the emission of hazardous substances on that site.

However, the notion of operator is variable, and in the end, certain natural or legal persons who are far removed from all operating activities have been qualified as operators by the law. One factor that has contributed greatly to the extension of liability beyond the owner or operator in the strict sense is the search for a waiver of the limitation of the shareholder's liability to the amount of his contributions, a search that is quite frequent in the United States, contrary to the European countries[15].

A. The parent company

The aim of the States has been to call into question the liability of the parent company, which is generally much more solvent than its subsidiary. The theory on which this questioning is based is that of the absence of real autonomy. The superfund law has brought the liability back on the owner, implicitly on the head of the parent company, whether or not the latter is the real polluter.

It must be recognized that the liability of the parent company has rarely been recognized in practice. An example of this can be found in US vs. Kayser-Roth Corporation.[16]

In this case, a textile manufacturer, a subsidiary of a parent company, had caused pollution of a Rhodes Island river by leaking a chemical (trichloroethylene) and by storing industrial products of this chemical.

The *Environmental Protection Agency had* to spend nearly a million dollars to restore the site, and brought an action against the parent company. The parent company was found to be the true operator, as the subsidiary was not independent of the parent company, thus

---

15 Patrick Thieffry, l'opportunité d'une responsabilité communautaire du pollueur; les distorsions entre les Etats membres et les enseignements de l'expérience américaine, RIDC, 1-1994, p.103, speculative. p.116.
16 US v. Kayser-Roth Corp. 724 F. Supp. 15 (D.R.I. 1989).

allowing it to be held liable.

However, this decision remains quite exceptional, and even if, in theory, the superfund law allows the parent company to be held liable, even though it had no influence in the decisions that caused the pollution of a site, practice shows that the risk of distortion of the polluter-pays principle to the detriment of the parent company is limited.

It may be pointed out that the European liability regime is not likely to be affected by this kind of distortion either, since it is not really in the European spirit to seek the liability of the parent company for the acts of a subsidiary.

B.   Individuals

The risk is really much greater for individuals who may be held personally liable under the C.E.R.C.L.A., which is frequently applied by federal jurisprudence[17] . According to this case law, an individual, a natural person, can be made to bear the burden of social activity.

However, there are two cumulative conditions that restrict the risk:

- the natural person must be a majority shareholder,

- and have management responsibilities in the company.

Case law has established that the manager can be exonerated if he or she proves that he or she had no part in the company's polluting activities, which therefore constitutes a serious obstacle to the questioning of managers.

C.   financiers

The definition of the operator or owner by the C.E.R.C.L.A. is simple. But in order to find absolutely solvent persons in charge, the jurisprudence has understood this definition in a very broad way, including the financiers of the polluting company.

Thus, a bank that has gone beyond the simple financing of the company (for example, by exercising rights it had over the mortgaged site[18]) may be declared liable.

It is clear from these developments that civil liability under the Superfund Act goes far beyond that of mere operators and owners, and the polluter pays principle itself. The search for a payer does not necessarily lead to the polluter, which is a serious infringement of the principle.

---

17 Kelley v. Thomas Solvant Co. 727 F. Supp. 1532 (W.D.Mich. 1989); State of New York vs. Shore Realty Corp. 759 F.2d 1032 (CA 2 1985); US vs. Conservation Chemical Co. 1215 (E.D. Ind. 1989); US vs. Mexico Feed and Steed Co. at 764 F. Supp. 565 (E.D. Mo. 1991).
18 US vs. Fleet factors Corp.911 F.2d 1550 (11th Cir. 1990).

§2 What causal link

The other important point of the superfund law for understanding what can be called its interpretation of the polluter-pays principle is the causal link.

This causal link is no longer necessary since 1975. A decision of the New York State Court of Appeals ruled that the current owner of a polluted site could be held liable, even if he was not the owner at the time of the pollution of the site, and that he did not cause the pollution[19].

In this case, a real estate developer had acquired land on which drums of toxic products, hazardous waste, and contaminated waste had been stored. The State of New York brought an action to require the developer to remediate the site. The developer argued that his property was posterior to the pollution in order to refuse to pay for remediation. But the federal court relied on the language of the C.E.R.C.L.A., holding that it was directed at current owners of polluted sites, not just the owners at the time of the pollution. The new owner of a polluted site can only be exonerated if he or she did not have the opportunity to know the state of pollution of the site. The judge considers that the new owner did not take the means to find out about the state of the site, and that he is therefore responsible for the pollution.

The developer was forced to pay for the treatment of 700,000 gallons of toxic chemicals, and hundreds of drums of hazardous and contaminated products.

This solution, in addition to causing an explosion in the number of environmental audits, seriously undermines legal certainty in that it does not at all respect the classic liability regime, nor even the polluter-pays principle, the principle underlying the origin of the C.E.R.C.L.A. law.

§3 Retroactivity

This insecurity is aggravated by the principle laid down in the C.E.R.C.L.A. law according to which it is retroactive. It can therefore be applied to pollution for which the generating event occurred prior to its entry into force.

Section 3: Critical Analysis

It is possible to find positive points in this law, at least financially. But the whole remains difficult to justify, as the negative consequences are numerous.

---

19 State of New-York v. Shore Realty Corp. 759 F. 2d. 1032 (CA 2 1985).

§1 The positive points of the law

This law is an excellent tool for finding solvent legal entities or individuals who can take over from the State in the restoration of sites. The declaration of responsibility is almost automatic: the notion of operator and owner is widely understood by the jurisprudence and by the law. The rehabilitation of sites is greatly facilitated, because those responsible can easily be required to repair the damage caused.

This solution of the American jurisprudence is also intended to avoid fraud. Indeed, in the event of pollution of a site, it would be too easy for a subsidiary to have to repair the damage caused during the exercise of its activity to resell the site to the parent company, or to another subsidiary of the parent company, with the responsibility for continuing to operate the site. In this way, if the operation is carried out several times, any restoration becomes impossible to obtain, as no responsible party can be found.

But it is easy to see that, in the end, the polluter-pays principle is no longer really present in the C.E.R.C.L.A. law.

§2 Negative points of the law

This positive point of the ease of finding a responsible person, more economic than legal, cannot make us forget all the flaws and defects of the system. Unfortunately, despite this earlier American example, these are the same flaws that the Green Paper will develop in Europe in 1993.

1° Distortion of the polluter-pays principle

The legal regime originally established was that of the polluter-payer. But we are witnessing a real distortion of the system: the polluter is not necessarily the payer, he may have no connection with the activity that caused the environmental damage, such as the new owner of a contaminated site.

2° The insurance crisis in the United States

The economic opportunism of this law has caused a number of disputes that have led to a serious insurance crisis in the United States[20] . Indeed, the lack of predictability as to the liability of companies, directors, and majority shareholders, the long delay between the event giving rise to the damage and the environmental damage, and the uncertainty as to the formation of a claim have been factors in the reluctance of the insurance industry to

---

20 Patrick Thieffry, Corporate Environmental Responsibility: European projects are becoming clearer, LPA, 21 February 2003, p.5.

offer services to companies, even though this service is already not very abundant[21] .

In the field of environmental damage compensation, insurance is a mandatory system for companies. For example, the German law provides for a compensation amount of up to 320,000,000 Deutschmarks[22] ! This amount is unsustainable for an uninsured company.

In addition, financial problems for companies were caused by this application of a superfund law regime that distorted the principles beyond reason, and prevented proper legal - and therefore financial - predictability.

<u>3° Inefficiency of the system</u>

Despite the application of this almost automatic liability system in the United States, remediation of polluted sites is not necessarily going faster than before. For example, in 2000, the number of registered polluted sites was 35,000. Only about 250 of them were rehabilitated[23] . At the same time, the number of disputes has exploded (although it has now stabilized).

Despite all the shortcomings of the American liability regime, the Europeans appreciated the superfund system because it made it easier to find a responsible party and to obtain compensation. They were therefore inspired by it to develop their liability regime in the event of environmental damage. They therefore based their environmental liability project solely on the polluter-pays principle. But, like the United States, their objective was more financial than legal. Their application of the polluter-pays principle has greatly distorted the latter.

---

21 Jean-Pierre Delvigne, La directive sur la responsabilité environnementale : une application du principe pollueur-payeur, DE, n°121, September 2004, p.163. And an example of this is given in Patrick Thieffry's article in the above-mentioned 1994 INCD, on page 121: German insurers limit coverage of damages to 20 million Deutschmarks, not even 10 percent of the maximum amount of compensation provided for under German law.
22 Patrick Thieffry, l'opportunité d'une responsabilité communautaire du pollueur; les distorsions entre les Etats membres et les enseignements de l'expérience américaine, RIDC, 1-1994, p.121.
23 Vincent Sol, Un droit en pleine évolution, LPA, 8 August 2000, n°157, p. 18.

Chapter 2: The liability regime envisaged by the Europeans

This regime can be found in the project of the Commission of the European Communities, called "Green Book". The purpose of this book is to elaborate a regime of liability for environmental damage. It is inspired by two texts, which are the draft Convention of the Council of Europe[24] on "civil liability for damage resulting from activities dangerous to the environment", and the proposal for a Community directive on "liability for damage caused to the environment by waste"[25] .

This system meets a genuine expectation of Community law (section 1). But the legal rules it lays down are open to criticism from the point of view of legal certainty (section 2).

Section 1: The reasons for the creation of a European liability regime

§1 The absence of Community law in this area

A.   <u>The multiplicity of texts with little coherence between them</u>

Prior to the Green Paper and its proposed regime of liability for environmental damage, environmental law was limited to a set of directives on specific subjects, which could not form a coherent whole.

For example, the Community has enacted texts on water protection - recast in 2000 -[26] , on wild birds[27] , on the ozone layer[28] , on "the conservation of natural habitats and of fauna and flora" (better known as the "Habitats" directive; this directive will be taken up by the 2004 directive on environmental liability)[29] .

However, article 130R of the Treaty of Rome as it results from the Single Act of 1986 has included the environment in the objectives of the EEC and then of the European Union.

---

24 Dated at that time December 4, 1992. This draft Convention became the Lugano Convention, adopted on 8 March 1993. It was opened for signature on 21 June 1993. However, this Convention has still not entered into force, as none of the three necessary ratifications have taken place to date. This refusal of the States to sign it is due to the excessive severity of the Convention, which sets very strict conditions of liability (see in particular Pascale Steichen, La proposition de directive du Parlement européen et du conseil sur la responsabilité environnementale en vue de la prévention et de la réparation des dommages environnementaux, RJ.E, February 2003, p.191, *in fine*).
Why do we focus more on the draft than on the Lugano Convention? The draft Convention and the Green Paper were thought out and elaborated at the same time. That is why the draft Convention can help to clarify the spirit of the environmental responsibility advocated by the European Community in the 1990s. But the Convention itself is of little interest to us.
25 Dated June 27, 1991.
26 Directive 2000/60 of the European Parliament and of the Council of 23 October 2000 on Community action in the field of water policy.
27 Council Directive 79-409 of 2 April 1979 on the conservation of wild birds, OJEC, No. L.103, 25 April 1979.
28 Regulation 309/94 of 15 December 1994, OJEC No. L.333 22 December 1994.
29 Directive of the European Parliament and of the Council of 21 May 1992 on the conservation of natural habitats and of wild fauna and flora, OJEC, No. L.206, 22 July 1992.

The environment has become an institutional matter that must be part of the fundamental policy of the Community. It should be emphasized that the environment is no longer seen as an element of the economy[30] . It is to be defended in parallel with the economy[31] , and a general and no longer piecemeal law is necessary.

<u>B.   The polluter pays principle, a European principle</u>

At the same time as it made the protection of the environment one of its fundamental objectives, the European Community established the economic principle of the polluter-pays as a legal principle: thus, Article 130R of the Treaty of Rome specifies that this protection of the environment is based on "the polluter-pays principle".

The first text that really takes up this principle is that of the draft Convention of the Council of Europe of 1992, the text that serves as a reference for the Green Paper. The draft uses this principle to justify the strict liability it implements. The explanatory report of this draft states: "The financial burden of this responsibility is passed on to the products and services that [the responsible operator] produces or provides, in accordance with the polluter-pays principle, which is considered by the international community to be a key principle in the field of environmental protection"[32] , confirming the fundamental nature of this principle for the European Union.

One of the interests of this report is that it reveals that the Council of Europe feels bound by the polluter-pays principle, not only because the Treaty of Rome establishes it as a fundamental principle, but also because the European Community itself is bound by the international community, which bases environmental protection on it ("(...) to the polluter-pays principle, which is considered by the international community to be a key principle"). This principle is for the Council the foundation par excellence of environmental law.

However, the polluter-pays principle was not originally conceived by the European Community as a basis for a liability regime. And its objective, when it cites it in Article 130R, is not that it be used in a liability regime. According to the OECD, it can only justify "compensation (...) or the financing of the repair of damage already done"[33] .

This polluter-pays principle is contrary to the search for the three traditional elements of liability regimes, namely, the cause, the damage, and the causal link, since its sole

---

30 Defending the environment independently of the economy does not prevent the Community from emphasizing that the two are nonetheless intimately linked, having consequences for each other. See in particular the Treaty of Amsterdam of 1999, on its policy on "Sustainable Development" (articles 2 and 6).
31 Articles 2 and 3 of the Treaty of Rome, as amended by the Treaty on European Union.
32 Explanatory Report of the Draft Convention, version of Dec. 4, 1992, No. 30, p. 29.
33 Draft OECD Recommendation of 2 April 1992 (on compensation to victims of accidental pollution, spec. no. 18).

purpose is to find out to whom to charge a cost.

This is precisely what the OECD says when it states that the polluter pays principle is an economic principle based on considerations of "opportunity" and economic "efficiency"[34] .

§2 Harmonizing European laws

A.   <u>What Europe says</u>

In addition to the inclusion of environmental protection in the Treaty of Rome to justify the creation of a general system of liability for environmental damage, the other reason invoked by the European institutions is that of the difference between the internal systems of the Member States[35] . According to her, European countries apply liability for fault in different ways, and she cites the example of France with the law of 15 July 1975.[36]

In their view, these differences are likely to cause a distortion of competition that could harm the establishment of the internal market.

B.   <u>Criticism of this desire to harmonize</u>

What is curious in the Green Paper is that, as Patrick Thieffry says[37] , this difference between internal laws is a reason explicitly invoked by the European institutions to justify their action, and at the same time, a description of the different regimes of the 12 Member States of 1992 is drawn up[38] , from which it is clear that the differences are rather minimal.

Moreover, the Green Paper recognizes this in its paragraph 2.2.1[39] : the legislation of the Member States for the protection of the environment converges and almost all of them respond to the principle of liability without fault.

<u>1° A minimal distortion of competition</u>

Moreover, while the commission explains that these differences in liability regimes result in a distortion of competition, it is also possible to question this reasoning.

---

34 Cf. the OECD study on "the polluter pays principle", published in 1992.

35Patrick Thieffry, L'opportunité d'une responsabilité communautaire du pollueur-payeur entre les Etats membres et les enseignements de l'expérience américaine, RIDC, 1994, p.106, note 11.

36 What is astonishing is that, in order to justify its reasoning, the European institution takes up only one of the existing French laws on ten, to draw the rather hasty conclusion that France applies in a general way for the protection of the environment the principle of liability for fault as it is presented in this 1975 law (Annex I, Green Book). This does not encourage one to take seriously the analyses of the Committee on European Legislation.

37 Patrick Thieffry, L'opportunité d'une responsabilité communautaire du pollueur-payeur entre les Etats membres et les enseignements de l'expérience américaine, RIDC, 1994, p. 106.

38 Annex I of the Green Paper.

39 Page 13 of the Green Book.

The commission's approach can be compared to its approach to product liability[40] .

To justify its action, the European Commission had pointed out that the liability regimes in the member countries of the Community were very divergent[41] .

However, this liability had undoubtedly negative repercussions on the economic laws of competition. The large proportion of mass-produced products that are actually defective and require repair, restoration or compensation, weighs heavily on the financial management of companies, and this differently depending on the liability regime preferred by the State. This justifies action to unify all the regimes for these products.

But for liability in case of environmental damage, it must be emphasized that the majority of industrial sites will not experience incidents with a serious consequence on the environment (fortunately!)[42] .

All of them will have an impact on the environment because of the very essence of their activity, which requires at least the use of natural resources and the release of materials into the biosphere (smoke, raw materials, waste, etc.). But for the most part, these impacts will not require large-scale remediation expenditures. The distortions of competition invoked by the European Commission are therefore unconvincing.

<u>2° The convergence of the legislations of the Member States</u>

It is true that there are differences between the laws of the Member States. However, it should be noted that the different liability regimes of these States converge towards the same regime: that of liability without fault.

For some years now, the States have had texts of a rather general scope which, for the most part, establish a presumption of fault. It should be noted that the jurisprudence of these countries is also moving towards no-fault liability[43] , without special texts. Finally, some of these texts do not even set out the concept of fault.

For example, the German law of December 10, 1990[44] on environmental liability establishes a presumption of fault for the operator of certain activities.

---

40 Directive 85/374 EEC of 25 July 1985 on product liability.

41 It is enough to compare the no-fault liability of the producer in French law and the English *negligence*).

42 Patrick Thieffry, L'opportunité d'une responsabilité communautaire du pollueur-payeur entre les Etats membres et les enseignements de l'expérience américaine, RIDC, 1994, p.103s.

43 Patrick Thieffry, L'opportunité d'une responsabilité communautaire du pollueur-payeur entre les Etats membres et les enseignements de l'expérience américaine, RIDC, 1994, p.103s.

44 German Environmental Liability Act of December 10, 1990, Bundesgesetzblatt, Part I, No. 67 of December 14, 1990, p. 2634.

The Greek law has adopted a regime similar to the German[45] for cases of pollution of industrial sites.

France and the United Kingdom have more or less the same regime for damage caused by waste disposed of by a person since the adoption of the English *Environmental Protection Act* of 1990[46] : they opt for the no-fault liability of the producer or the carrier. Their jurisprudence on the subject also leads to a greater severity towards the producer, the operator or the carrier.

In the United Kingdom, the case that best demonstrates the evolution of case law towards greater severity in establishing the liability of the polluter is the 1992 *Cambridge Water Company* decision.

The Cambridge Water Company jurisprudence broadens the liability cases as accepted for nearly 150 years in pollution cases[47] . According to this case law, the pollution of a natural resource by the operator of a site interferes with the natural right of the users of that resource.

In this case, a tannery, *Eastern Counties Leatherwork Plc.* had spilled chemicals on a site, resulting in the pollution of the groundwater below. The *Cambridge Water Company, a* user of the groundwater, went to court to seek redress, which was granted, for the tanner's encroachment on the *Company*'s natural right. And this even though the use of the toxic products in question was lawful.

As for French jurisprudence, it is increasingly extending the no-fault liability regime (for example, with the exoneration for force majeure, which has been reduced to a minimum).

The Netherlands and Belgium do not even mention the notion of fault. Belgium provides that the producer of toxic waste is liable for any damage, whatever its nature and whatever its cause[48] .

The Netherlands has adopted soil protection legislation that makes operators of hazardous

---

45 Article 29 of the Greek law n°1650 of October 16, 1986.
46 *Environmental Protection Act*, Section 73-6.
47 *Rylands vs. Fletcher*, 1868. In this judgment, the conditions for the liability of the operator of a site were rather restrictive; the occupier of the land was only liable for damages caused by "the emission of toxic substances if their presence on the land did not correspond to the natural destination of the said place", which is restrictive, since it means that: 1. the substance must be introduced on the land, 2. this is not the natural destination of the site, and 3. the substance escapes. This judgment is very revealing of the spirit of the 19th century and the will to protect industrial progress above all, in spite of the environment. L.R. 3 HL 330.
48 Belgian Law of 22 July 1974; Bocken, "la réparation des dommages causés par la pollution en droit belge", R.G.D.C., 1992, p. 284.

activities liable regardless of the cause of the damage, whether they are at fault or not[49] .

It is therefore a real no-fault liability that has been decided in these countries. It is visible that the Member States in general are moving towards a no-fault liability in the protection of the environment.

All these examples leave one wondering why the Green Paper was adopted. It claims to harmonize European laws on environmental liability, whereas the study of these laws shows that they converge towards the same type of regime.

As the Green Paper points out, it is nevertheless true that there are distortions in European laws, and the arrival of new members in the European Union, bringing the number of member states to 25, has not failed to reinforce them. All the more so as some of them have a much less developed awareness of the environment than the old members of the European Union[50] , while they have a much greater number of historical pollutions[51] (such as the countries of the former USSR, whose industrial development is less, which encourages them to prefer to develop their industries first, before defending the environment).

However, these distortions were not such as to justify an intervention of the European Commission in 1993, as the Member States were all moving towards the same type of liability, liability without fault.

C.   The omissions of European law

The justification is all the more difficult to understand since the draft provides for the freedom of States on certain legal points: the environmental protection measures provided for "shall not prevent any Member State from maintaining or introducing more stringent protective measures" (Article 130T of the Treaty)[52] . However, these points are crucial to the defence of the environment.

One thinks of developmental risks, causation, and reparation.

1° Development risks

None of the three texts proposed by the European institutions address the problem of

---

49 *Interim Soil Protection Act* of 1982, and *Soil Protection Act* of 1986. In both of these *Acts*, liability is based on the hazardous nature of the activity.

50 Barbara Jesus-Gimeno, Protection of the environment through criminal law, for a community approach, Environment, May 2002, p.8.

51 Pascale Steichen, La proposition de directive du Parlement européen et du conseil sur la responsabilité environnementale en vue de la prévention et de la réparation des dommages environnementaux, RJ.E, February 2003, p.177

52 It is obvious that the *sine qua non* condition is that these measures are compatible with the measures of the treaty.

development risks; the proposed directive on waste liability does not mention it, nor does the green paper.

The solution proposed by the Council of Europe Convention on Civil Liability for Damage resulting from Activities Dangerous to the Environment risks causing even more distortion, since it leaves the possibility for States to regulate themselves the legal situation of these development risks: it is possible for any Member State to "provide in its domestic law (') that the state of scientific and technical knowledge at the time of the event did not allow for knowledge of the existence of the dangerous properties of the substance or of the significant risk that the operation presented to the organism"[53] .

The two other sensitive points in a liability regime are those of causation and reparation.

2° The repair

The question of reparation consists mainly in knowing how the compensation will be calculated: should it only take into account the reparation of material damage, or should it include compensation for moral damage? Should there be a ceiling on compensation or should it be left to the sovereignty of the judge?

These questions are essential because, as has already been pointed out, the costs of environmental damage can be very high. In this case, multiple solutions have been adopted in the member countries.

For example, Germany, by its law of December 10, 1990, excludes any compensation for moral prejudice. However, it admits full compensation for material damage, with the establishment of ceilings[54] for compensation.

Moreover, the jurisdictions have different visions of personal injury, which can lead to very varied reparations (assuming that the law in question accepts the compensation of moral injury). The same is true for ecological damage.

3° The causal link

For the causal link, the question arises as to whether countries will prefer to opt for an irrebuttable presumption of a causal link between the polluting activity and the damage, or whether this link will have to be really sought by the parties. Will they be able to demonstrate, as in German law, that another circumstance is the cause of the damage[55] ?

---

53 Article 35, paragraph 1 (b) of the Council of Europe Convention as of December 4, 1992.
54 160,000,000 deutschemarks for personal injury and 160,000,000 deutschemarks for property damage. A total of 320,000,000; article 15 of the law of December 10, 1990.
55 Article 7 of the German law of 10 December 1990.

In addition, the no less important question on the subject concerns the cases of exoneration, with the question of whether force majeure and the fault or act of the victim will be accepted. (Most states today accept the demonstration of fortuitous event, or the victim's act).[56]

In addition to these questions, which concern the substantive problems of the legal system of environmental protection, there are questions that are perhaps more formal, but certainly just as essential: the procedure and its length, the methods of establishing proof (including possible state aid in the search for evidence, for example). These questions of form are the main factor of distortion of European law.

These numerous, but not exhaustive, examples show that the desire to harmonize European laws displayed by the European institutions is not a *priori a* real reason. The distortions that it leaves, and at the same time the natural harmonization of the different European laws, do not lead to take seriously the reasons invoked by the Commission.

On the other hand, the international dimensions of environmental problems are likely to play a major role in the establishment of a liability regime.

The European Council has already had occasion to stress the international nature of these problems, and current events have repeatedly reminded us that environmental damage knows no borders[57] .

As we have seen with the analysis of article 130R of the Treaty of Rome, the Council of Europe, in its Explanatory Report of 4 December 1992 on its draft Convention, relies on the international character of environmental protection as the basis for its action.

Section 2: The regime proposed by the Green Paper

The Green Paper, which proposes a liability regime applicable to all damage caused to the environment, bases its regime on the one hand on a compensation fund, and on the other hand on strict liability.

§ 1   The compensation fund

A.   <u>The concept of the compensation fund</u>

It consists in taxing potential polluters, the sum thus collected allowing the repair of all the damage caused to the environment for which the true responsible party would not be

---

56 For example, *the* United Kingdom's *Environmental Protection Act* of 1990, or Greece's Law No. 1650 of 1986, Article 29.

57 For example: Chernobyl in 1986, the pollution of the Rhine in 1986 by the fire of a pesticide factory and in 1995, the air pollution, the maritime pollution of the Amoco Cadiz of March 16, 1978, of the Erika of December 11, 1999.

found. This avoids the State having to intervene itself, at least in the repair of the damage.

It obviously originates from the American superfund, whose positive effect on Europe was to avoid making the State responsible for the repair or restoration of the environment.

Even if the Commission was inspired by American law to create its compensation fund, the system already exists in European countries, where some states already levy taxes in anticipation of repairing environmental damage.

Some of these levies or taxes are done on the polluters who use certain products known to harm the environment. That is to say on potential polluters. Others are levied on the actual polluters recognized as such by the local administrations.

One example is France, where levies have been in place for several years.

A tax has existed since the beginning of environmental protection in France, with the "water pollution tax" of the 1964 law[58] . It is levied on public and private persons who are recognized as effective water polluters.

In addition to this fee, there is the parafiscal tax of 31 December 1992 on noise pollution caused by aircraft[59] . It can be seen that this last fee corresponds well to the current spirit of broadening the types of environmental nuisance to other types of nuisance than material nuisance (noise nuisance).

Potential polluters are levied the "single tax" and the annual fee on classified installations provided for by the law of 17 July 1976[60] . This tax and fee are payable by the operators of installations that pose particular risks to the environment.

Finally, as a last example, there is the parafiscal tax levied on certain lubricants provided for by the decree of 31 August 1989[61] . The purpose of this tax is to allow the collection of used oils and their disposal.

All these examples show that a European levy system would not completely upset the current legal landscape, where such a form of damage compensation has already been thought of.

These taxes and charges are payable by potential and actual polluters. It has been sought to associate this fund with a strict liability regime. However, they are legally different.

---

58 December 16, 1964.
59 Section 16s. of Law 92-1444 of December 31, 1992 (D. and ALD. 1993.106).
60 Article 17 of the law of 17 July 1976.
61 Decree 89-648 of August 31, 1989 for the benefit of the ADEME (Agency for the Environment and Energy Management) created by a law n°90-1130 on December 19, 1990.

<u>B.</u>   <u>The difference between these levies and a liability regime</u>

Both operate within a logic inspired by this type of liability, namely that polluters are responsible for the damage they cause to the environment, whatever the reason for the pollution, whatever the extent of their actual liability.

But this does not mean that these levies can be equated with a strict liability regime.

The payment of levies is not subject to the establishment of a link between the damage and the activity (or the materials, such as used oil), and above all does not depend on the victim and his legal remedies. Thus, it has been written that "the perspective in which the polluter intervenes is displaced [in the case of the polluter-pays principle and in that of pollution charges] (...). It is no longer subject to the hazards of jurisdictional actions subsequent to the damage. It intervenes preventively to organize the redistribution of costs among the various economic actors"[62] .

It is impossible to confuse these levies, and any compensation fund, with strict liability, which is the second point of the Commission's proposed regime.

§2 The objective responsibility set up by the Green Paper

<u>A.</u>   <u>Which managers</u>

The people concerned by these measures are professionals, and this for all European projects.

Thus in its article 1er -1, the draft directive provides that liability will be incurred for "damage and degradation of the environment caused by waste generated in the course of a professional activity".

Similarly, the draft Council Convention on Damage Resulting from Activities Dangerous to the Environment provides that "the operator of a dangerous activity ... shall be liable for damage caused by that activity resulting from events occurring at the time or during the period when he exercised control over it" (Article 6-1). The Convention provides an exhaustive list of the hazardous activities it covers in Article 2-1, all of which are occupational activities.

<u>B.</u>   <u>What damage to the environment</u>

How is this environment understood in the draft directive on environmental law?

<u>1° The definition of the environment</u>

---

62 Dupuy, La responsabilité internationale des Etats pour dommages technologiques et industriels, Pedone, 1976.

The European Council's draft Convention defines in its article 2-7 the damage to which it applies as "any loss or damage resulting from the alteration of the environment [which cannot be considered as constituting material or physical damage]", and defines the environment as "the abiotic and biotic natural resources, such as air, water, soil, fauna and flora, and the interaction between the same factors, the property that makes up the cultural heritage and the characteristic aspects of the landscape" (article 2-10).

This definition is very precise and is distinguished by its quality.

The absence of a definition of the environment in the Green Paper is all the more surprising. The Convention is intended to apply only to a part of the environment and gives a very precise definition of it. The draft, on the other hand, applies to the whole of the environment, and yet gives no definition of its purpose. The commission merely said that the damage could be chemical, physical or biological, as long as the damage was to the environment.

Without a definition of the environment, it can be understood in many ways. It can be understood as including all natural resources; to these resources can be added the notions of landscape, biosphere, these definitions having significant financial consequences.

<u>2° Damage</u>

Environmental damage can be of two kinds, and it is important to distinguish between them in order to understand an environmental liability regime.

Environmental damage can be understood either as damage to people and things, or as physical and material damage. In the latter case, the environment is a vector through which the pollution causes harm to the environment in which the victims live.

Damage can also be understood as damage to the environment alone, taken as an entity. In this case, the damage taken into account is really what is called an attack on the environment, an attack on "pure ecological" interests, independently of an attack on individual rights"[63] . The right thus created could then approach a true environmental right.

Both types of damage are environmental damage, and the Green Paper chose to consider all of these types of damage.

This solution is also the one favored by the American C.E.R.C.L.A. law, which takes into

---

63 Isabelle Doussan, Le droit de la responsabilité civile française à l'épreuve de la " responsabilité environnementale " instaurée par la directive du 21 avril 2004, LPA, p.3.

account all damages caused by pollution[64] .

In the European projects, such as the Green Paper, a draft directive on environmental law in general, and the draft directive on damage caused by waste of 1991, the damage caused is each time taken in a total way, i.e. both physical and material damage, as well as damage to the environment *stricto sensu*.

The Green Paper also admits that pre-existing damage may be covered. This way of admitting the definition of a damage represents well what Europe basically wants: it would like to create a right that would allow to find a person responsible for pollution in general, to find a payer for the damage. It does not matter what the object of this damage is.

The interest of this conception of damage is that it makes it possible to give all the damage arising from the same origin the same system of reparation. It would indeed be unacceptable for damage to the environment *stricto sensu to* be compensated through the application of a no-fault liability regime, whereas damage to human beings, including damage to health, would be left to the victim, through the application of a fault-based liability regime[65] . This is, moreover, what had interested the Europeans when they read the regime of objective liability set up by the C.E.R.C.L.A. law.

Thus, the damages caused to the man are included in the framework of the green book. That is to say all the damages to his health, to his property, or to his activities.

By including human activities, the commission has included non-profit activities. But how can the damage to a non-profit activity be compensated? Restoration would not be sufficient, since the damage must include the impediment to the activity that the pollution has caused for a time. It is also possible that the damage to the activity is irreversible.

How to calculate such a prejudice, knowing that the activity did not bring any income or turnover to the operator? Yet it is indeed a prejudice.

The damage included in the subject matter of the directive is also damage to the lucrative activities of man, in other words commercial damage. For example, the pollution of a river by chemicals may cause a loss of productivity to a cereal field, for which the farmer may claim compensation at the same time as the restoration of the river.

This agricultural damage is a direct consequence of the environmental damage, but it

---

64 See Title 1, Chapter 1, Section 1, §1
65 Especially since the social role of repairing these damages to the environment or by the environment is not to be neglected, especially in the case of damages to health.

cannot be assimilated to it[66] .

In so doing, the directive moves away from a real environmental law. It only focuses on the notion of the polluter-payer, forgetting what the law it intends to apply in the Member States should be about.

In a sense, it prefers to regulate the regime of damage caused by pollution, but not really to create an environmental law. And yet, it is the objective of the Green Paper to create an environmental law!

There is also a fundamental difference between accidental damage and chronic damage. This difference is very important because it has major legal and financial consequences[67] .

Accidental damage is damage that happens unpredictably, chronic damage is diffuse damage.

However, the draft directive and the draft convention do not distinguish between them, applying the polluter-pays principle to both.

However, the absence of differentiation between damages can have particularly harmful consequences for insurance, and therefore *a fortiori* for the compensation of these damages.

<u>3° The problem of chronic pollution</u>

Originally, the polluter-pays principle was only created for the protection of the environment in the face of chronic pollution, in order to share the burden of the costs of this pollution among the various polluters. The polluter-pays principle only seemed to be adapted to chronic pollution[68] , pollution which, because of the uncertainties it generates, cannot be subject to the traditional liability regime.

Indeed, chronic damage is characterized by its progressive nature. This progressive character is manifested in time and space.

Chronic pollution initially has little impact on the environment. It occurs insidiously and is first absorbed by the environment. When the environment is saturated, the pollution appears, unfortunately often already irreversible. This delay between the pollution and its declaration makes it impossible to determine exactly when the damage was caused.

---

66 Christian Larroumet, La responsabilité civile en matière d'environnement. Le projet de Convention du Conseil de l'Europe et le livre vert de la Commission des Communautés Européennes, Dalloz 1994, p. 101.
67 Christian Larroumet, *op.cit*, spec. p.102.
68 H. Smets, le principe pollueur-payeur, un principe économique érigé en principe de droit de l'environnement, RGDI *publ.* 1993.339.

The result is uncertainty as to when the damage is certain, and inevitably as to when an action for damages can be brought.

In space, chronic pollution spreads widely without it being possible to determine the exact extent of this pollution (rivers, groundwater, atmosphere, especially since the lack of knowledge of the time of the pollution makes it impossible to realize which damage has really been caused by the pollution in question, and which was present before).

These uncertainties also make it difficult to determine whether the pollutions originate from the same responsible party, or whether there are multiple responsible parties.

Since it cannot be subject to the liability regime because of the uncertainty attached to it, the only way to allow the repair of chronic pollution is to subject this type of damage to the polluter-pays principle[69] .

Accidental damages seem to be the only ones suitable for the liability regime. However, it is necessary to distinguish between actual accidental damage and potential accidental damage which cannot be subject to the liability regime. Indeed, their nature prevents the three basic elements of liability from being sought, especially the causal link. For these types of damage, if we want to make the polluters bear the cost of prevention and restoration of the natural environment, we must apply the polluter-pays principle. With the negative consequences that this has for the insurance system.

A clarification seems necessary here. The accident, which should be the cause of the damage, consists of a sudden and instantaneous event. But this does not mean that the damage which results from the accident must also occur suddenly. A pollution damage, even if it is accidental, can still be gradual. The suddenness must relate to its cause, not its occurrence. For example, cracks in a pipe that allow chemicals to escape into a river make the pollution typically gradual. But the cause of the pollution is accidental, unforeseeable.

In fact, accidental and unforeseeable are closely linked[70] . The notion of accident therefore means rather that the fact at the origin of the damage must be unforeseeable, unlike the facts of chronic pollution which are foreseeable and even sometimes programmed.

The other essential point of the liability regime is the causal link between the damage and the harmful act.

<u>C.</u>   <u>The causal link</u>

---

69 H. Smets, the polluter-pays principle, an economic principle established as a principle of environmental law, RGDI *publ.* 1993.339

70 Christian Larroumet, La responsabilité civile en matière d'environnement. Le projet de Convention du Conseil de l'Europe et le livre vert de la Commission des Communautés Européennes, Dalloz 1994, p. 105.

This causal link is what connects the damage and the act of another. The major part of the search for proof is therefore often based on this element of the liability regime.

The flexibility of the liability regime depends on the broad acceptance of proof of causation.

In the case of environmental damage caused by companies, it is sometimes difficult to demonstrate that there was a link between the activity and the damage observed on the environment.

For example, how do you prove that industrial activity at a site is responsible for the decline in the variety of the biosphere in the region, especially when the damage occurs after a long period of time?

To make a liability regime more favourable to one party or another, it is sufficient to relax or rigidify the causal link.

In the American superfund regime, the causal link is understood in a flexible way, so that the regime is more favourable to the victims. In practice, in this law, the causal link is no longer necessary, since even new owners who had no part in the activities that caused the pollution can be considered liable.

The draft Convention on Civil Liability for Damage resulting from Hazardous Activities and the Commission's Green Paper have the same conception of the causal link. The draft Convention provides in its Article 10 that "when assessing the evidence relating to the causal link between the event and the damage, the judge shall take due account of the increased risk of causing the damage inherent in the dangerous activity".

The Commission proposes much the same thing, since its draft proposes a presumption of causality between the damage and the activity "likely by its nature" to be the cause of that damage.

However, while the draft Convention defines hazardous activities in Article 2-1, the activities "likely by their nature" to cause damage in the Commission's Green Paper do not. The Green Paper is therefore not precise enough. In addition to this lack of precision, the two proposals take liberties with the legal regime of the causal link.

Legally, this solution advocated by these projects is a denaturation of the causal link. This causal link no longer has to be proven. The objective of this system is to facilitate the search for proof for the victim of the damage, and for a payer, in line with the polluter-pays principle.

Of course, the treaty leaves the member states free to choose the system they consider appropriate for determining the causal link. However, the principle of subsidiarity does not allow them to deviate from the regime proposed by the European texts. Therefore, the Member States will necessarily opt for a flexible system for determining causality.

<u>D.</u>   <u>liability action and payment</u>

The environment is a *res communis* that has no owner and no personality.

The question then arises as to who can act in liability for disturbance of this *res communis*?

For the sake of legal certainty, it is essential to determine who can act, i.e. who has an interest in acting.

The problem is that the environment, which is the only one concerned by the reparation, does not have legal personality; it is neither a legal person nor a natural person, and therefore cannot be represented.

It has been proposed to give the environment a legal personality, which would have made it a direct victim of the damage[71] . But many authors, such as Christian Larroumet, have virulently opposed this solution[72] .

The environment is a true *res communis*, that is, it belongs to no one. It is not the sum of several particular prejudices, like the prejudices of various properties that would be added to each other. Belonging to no one, it is truly part of the general interest, and a prejudice caused to it is a collective prejudice in the most absolute sense of the term.

The combination of individual actions cannot therefore be considered as an action to repair damage to the environment. For the group action is only the sum of individual actions; it is therefore better to rule out this type of action for the defense of the environment. This is the idea developed by the Commission's Green Paper.

On the other hand, perhaps it is possible to entrust approved associations for the defense of the environment with the power to take action to repair damage. Some associations already exist, and already have judicial prerogatives. However, this solution has the great disadvantage of favouring the multiplicity of actions, for one and the same prejudice.

Indeed, a pollution can have repercussions on multiple aspects of the environment, each one defended by an association. Thus, a prejudice will have the effect of multiplying the

---

71 Christian Huglo, "Vers la reconnaissance d'un droit de la nature à réparation", Petites Affiches, 29 September 1993, n° 117, p. 15.
72 Christian Larroumet, Dalloz 1994, supra, pp. 106 and 107.

actions of associations which will all invoke an interest to act.

The multiplication of actions is not desirable. Especially since the multiplication of these actions poses a problem as to the organization of the distribution of the sums allocated for reparation.

It therefore seems desirable to entrust the power to act to the public authorities, who would act either through the public prosecutor's office or through a public body. Obviously, the approved associations could intervene with the authorized body.

The question also arises as to whether an action is possible in the event that reparation is not possible? The action brought can only be an action for reparation, it cannot be, for example, an action for damages to the environment. So if any reparation is unthinkable, no action should be brought. This is a delicate solution, but at the same time it is the fairest solution from a legal point of view, since it would best respect the rights of the polluting party, without encroaching on those of the plaintiff. Indeed, the polluting party would not pay for a remedy that is impossible to execute. And the rights of the plaintiff would not be violated, as the absence of an award is only due to the impossibility of repair[73] .

This is the solution expressly adopted by the Council's draft Convention, which defines damage in terms of reparation in its article *2-7 c* (if there is no reparation, there is legally no damage. This is the same principle as in criminal law, where the offence is defined in terms of the penalty).

E.   <u>The risk of an insurance crisis</u>

But even with the application of classical liability to accidental damage, the special character of environmental protection can cause a crisis in insurance. This risk should be taken into account by the European institutions, it cannot be left aside. The example of the application of the American C.E.R.C.L.A. law shows that a liability regime in environmental matters must absolutely take into account the consequences that this regime could have for insurance.

It does not seem legally shocking to establish the principle of liability for environmental damage in the context of the *normal* exercise of an activity, provided that this activity is of a professional nature, as specified in the draft directive on pollution by waste (article 1[er] -1 and 2-1), and the draft Council Convention.

---

73 It may be objected that the impossibility of repair should not be an obstacle to awarding a sum for environmental repair: this sum could very well be used for the restoration of other polluted sites. But is it fair to make a company pay for repairs to pollution that it did not even cause? This is hardly justifiable.

Indeed, there are legal precedents for the establishment of liability for the normal exercise of one's rights. The most obvious is obviously the "troubles anormaux du voisinage" of French law, where liability can arise during the normal and regular exercise of an activity.

Legally, the normal exercise of an activity can lead to liability. But this runs up against the general principle of insurance law. This principle is that damage is only insured if it occurs as a result of a random event, such as an accident or unintentional fault.

That is, if it is unpredictable.

"Insurance can only be applied from the moment when the damaging event constitutes a hazard. It must be a phenomenon that occurs without the knowledge of its author, excluding all damage resulting from polluting activities that continue in a constant and deliberate manner"[74] .

The OECD states the same thing in its report when it says that damage from necessarily polluting activities is not covered by insurance[75] .

It is clear that this is not the liability system advocated today. Not only does it contravene the founding legal principle of insurance, but it may also lead to an insurance crisis, such as occurred in the United States in the 1980s.

With insurance companies withdrawing, this could leave companies with an immense financial burden as they are left with exorbitant environmental rehabilitation costs that they cannot bear alone.

Especially since the environment is taken as a whole, as *res communis*, and not just as the 'sum' of properties[76] . In which case the rehabilitations would take place only for the biosphere, the landscapes, the natural resources of the properties. But here, the rehabilitation takes place for the whole environment, whether man has a hold on it or not, which can extend almost infinitely the natures and extents of the rehabilitation measures.

The deficits of the regime towards which the European Community was moving are well known. The system that was supposed to be a legal liability system is in fact a financial system. There are numerous infringements of the law: reparations, generating event, causal link. The polluter-pays principle itself is not respected by the Commission. The payer and the polluter are clearly distinguished, even if this distinction is less marked than in the American superfund law.

---

74 G. Husson, le point de vue des assureurs, *in Le dommage écologique en droit interne, communautaire et comparé*, Economica, 1992, p. 179.
75 Monographies sur l'environnement, n° 42, *L'assurance pollution*, 1992, p.7, in note.
76 H.W. Hoffman, La responsabilité civile pollution et son assurance en Allemagne, RGAT, 1992.474.

The Green Paper largely accepts the notion of damage, seeming to forget that its objective is originally a regime of environmental liability, which does not include damage caused to objects other than the environment.

And the environment itself is not defined.

All these notorious shortcomings are due to the spirit that originally prevailed in the Community, which was to find a payer for the damage. Today, the Commission is breaking with this logic.

Second Title : The recent evolution of the European liability regime for environmental damage

Directive n°2004/35 of 21 April 2004 on liability with regard to the prevention and remedying of environmental damage is a far cry from the gloomy prospects that its gestation in the Green Paper might have raised. The essential objective of the obligations envisaged is the protection of the environment by preventing damage or restoring it to its original state, and this objective clearly takes precedence over any concern for the implementation of the polluter-pays principle. This principle no longer plays a rigid role in the implementation of the regime.

The directive returns to an application of the theory of fault, with the establishment of an original system of liability (chapter 1). However, the directive undoubtedly does not yet go far enough in its reflection with regard to the parallel evolution of liability for damage caused to the environment, visible in other European or internal texts. It could undoubtedly have better integrated the idea of fault, and especially taken into account contractual relations (chapter 2).

Chapter 1: The principles developed in European law by the 2004 directive

Over time and under pressure from business (section 1), the European Union has finally returned to a more legally compliant environmental liability regime (section 2). However, this regime requires certain corrections (section 3).

Section 1 : Why this change of direction

After the publication of the Green Paper, many companies undertook a vast lobbying campaign in Brussels, which lasted nearly fifteen years, to have the measures deemed too penalizing for them withdrawn[77] .

They have succeeded in having a number of measures withdrawn, such as charging them for pre-existing damage, and presuming causation.

In addition, and more pragmatically, international pressure on the subject has diminished. At the beginning of the 1990's, the States and the international organizations became aware of the dangers linked to an ever increasing pollution, and especially to the extent of the consequences on the international level. Solemn and energetic declarations followed[78] , and legislation was radical in the protection of the environment, to the point of forgetting the principle of legal certainty, as we have seen with the American C.E.R.C.L.A. law.

Today, the European Community has taken a step back. It is true that the question arises as to why the Community has not learned from the American C.E.R.C.L.A. and its defects in order to develop its own system, even though many authors have advocated taking them into account[79] .

That said, even if the Commission did not seem to be inspired by the American model, the directive really does move away from its pitfalls, which the Green Paper did not seem to have seen, as it took up the same principles as the law across the Atlantic.

Section 2 The legal system chosen by the Commission

---

77 Patrick Thieffry, La directive sur la responsabilité environnementale enfin adoptée, LPA, 21 May 2004, n°102, p.5; and from the same author, Responsabilité environnementale des entreprises, les projets européens se précisent, LPA, 21 February 2003, p.4.

78 For example, the UNESCO declaration of November 1989 in Vancouver, entitled the "Vancouver Declaration on Survival in the 21st Century"; *op.cit.*

79 See in particular Vincent Sol, Sanctions et responsabilités en droit de l'environnement : l'expérience américaine, RDAI, n°7, 1993, p.869 ; Christian Larroumet, La responsabilité civile en matière d'environnement. Le projet de Convention du Conseil de l'Europe et le livre vert de la Commission des Communautés européennes, Dalloz 1994, chron. p.101 ; Patrick Thieffry, La directive dur la responsabilité environnementale enfin adoptée, RIDC, 1994, p.103.

The directive sought to create an important regime of prevention of environmental damage. Although it constitutes the major part of the directive, it will be treated exclusively of the part on the repair.

Damage can be repaired if it affects the environment as defined in the directive. But the damage itself must have a particular nature. Indeed, the directive differentiates the types of damage according to the resources that are affected by the pollution. Each resource thus receives "its" own definition of damage.

§1 The field of repair

A.   The definition of the environment

The main defect of the Green Paper was that it established a liability regime for damage caused to the environment, but without defining the content of this environment. The directive has made up for this absence and has defined the field of application of this liability.

However, it would not be fair to say that the directive defines the environment. Rather, it defines what part of the environment it wants to protect. For example, no reference is given to the atmosphere, a natural part of the environment. But this definition is still commendable, because it avoids the legal vagueness that dominated the Green Paper. The area of responsibility is now known.

Unlike the Convention's draft, which defines the environment without reference to previous texts[80] , the 2004 Environmental Liability Directive is based on numerous directives previously adopted by the European Union.

This environment includes soils and subsoils, waters, species and natural habitats.

1° The biosphere

For damage to species and natural habitats, the directive refers to the directives of 2 April 1979 on the conservation of wild birds[81] and of 21 May 1992 on the conservation of natural habitats and of wild flora and fauna[82] . It should be noted in passing that under the "birds" directive, the States must create special protection areas (SPAs) and, under the "habitats" directive, special conservation areas (SACs). All these areas together constitute the "Natura 2000" zone. This zoning is the one according to which is determined the domain of the damage to the environment that can be repaired according to the regime established

---

80 Article 2-7 and Article 2-10 of the draft convention, *op.cit.*
81 Directive n° 79/409 of April 2, 1979, O.J.C.E. n°L 103 of April 29, 1979.
82 Directive n°92/43 of May 21, 1992, OJEC n° L 206 of July 22, 1992.

by the directive.

To these areas may be added those chosen by the Member States for purposes similar to those of the directive[83] . That is to say that biodiversity is also defined by reference to national legislation for the protection of habitats and species. In our environmental code, article L.411-1 provides for the protection of animal and plant species, the list of which is fixed by decree.

The protection here is directly related to the species, by prohibiting their destruction or degradation, but without creating a specific zoning that would be likely to integrate the community responsibility system.

This zoning in France can only result from biotope decrees, decrees established with the help of scientific documents[84] . In France, the directive also applies to national parks[85] , regional parks[86] , nature reserves, protected forests, state and forest biological reserves, sensitive natural areas in the departments[87] , sites acquired by the Conservatoire du littoral et des rives lacustres, and the N zones of local urban planning schemes.

Thus, the scope of the directive goes far beyond that of its provisions; it includes a number of internal provisions that may be subject to the liability regime that the directive establishes.

<u>2° Water, soil and subsoil</u>

For damage affecting water, the 2004 directive refers to the directive of 23 October 2000, which establishes a Community framework in the field of water policy, "with the exception of negative impacts to which article 4, paragraph 7, of the said directive applies"[88] . The waters concerned are all surface, groundwater, coastal and transitional waters.

For soil damage, the directive does not refer to a specific text.

The directive explicitly excludes damage to the atmosphere.

---

83 Jean-Pierre Delvigne, La directive sur la responsabilité environnementale, une application du principe pollueur-payeur, Droit de l'Environnement n° 121, September 2004.
84 These decrees are issued without a public inquiry by the prefect and set out measures to promote, in all or part of the department, the conservation of biotopes insofar as they are necessary for the feeding, reproduction, resting or survival of species protected under interministerial decrees (art. R. 211-12 to R. 211-14 of the Rural Code). The local or regional inventories on which these decrees are based have no real normative scope. See M. Prieur, "Droit de l'Environnement", Dalloz, 4th edition, p. 404.
85 Article L.331-1 of the Environment Code.
86 Article L.333-1 of the Environment Code.
87 Article L.332-1 of the Environment Code, to which must be added the reserves of the law n°2002-276 of February 27, 2002, on local democracy. All the same, these reserves cover today more than 552 000 hectares.
88 Directive 2000/60 of 23 October 2000, OJEC No. L 237 of 22 December 2000.

And this for the reason that it wants to take into account only the certain and well determined damages. However, by the very nature of their object, atmospheric pollutions are not determinable, they are too diffuse.

Damage is only covered if it affects these areas of biosphere, water, soil and subsoil as defined in the directive. But they must also have a certain form. Not all damage to these resources can be the subject of a liability procedure.

B.   The nature of the damage

(1) the damages repaired

The notion of damage is first given a general definition, but then the directive specifies the nature that the damage must have for each of the resources mentioned above.

The definition of damage is quite precise: damage is "a measurable negative change in a natural resource and/or a measurable deterioration of a service related to natural resources, which may occur directly or indirectly and which is caused by any activity covered by the directive". The notion of "service" is defined as "the functions provided by a natural resource for the benefit of another natural resource and/or the public".

Economic damage is not considered to be part of the scope of the directive, as is clear from article 3, paragraph 8: "(...) this directive does not confer on the parties any right to compensation for any economic loss they may have suffered as a result of environmental damage or an imminent threat of such damage".

The economic damage suffered by a fisherman because of the pollution of a river will not be compensated, unlike the initial project, that of the 1993 Green Paper, which included in the damages all the economic losses suffered by the people exploiting the natural resources.

The directive specifies the definitions of damage by differentiating between resources.

Damage affecting biodiversity will only be taken into account if it "seriously and adversely affects the conservation status of biodiversity". It is the character of seriousness that is added here compared to the general definition.

The state of the water can only be repaired if the negative consequences of the pollution on its quality make it leave one of the categories of the directive n°2000/60/CE[89] . The state of the water is classified according to three categories, very good, good, and

---

89 Except for the adverse effects to which the provisions of article 4, paragraph 7 of this directive n° 2000/60/EC are applied.

average. This means that if the water goes down one category, or even out of the categories given in Annex V of the directive, a remedy can be ordered[90] .

Soil and subsoil damage is understood to be that which may cause a risk of serious negative impact on human health or natural resources due to the direct or indirect introduction of substances, preparations, organisms or micro-organisms on the surface or in the soil[91] .

Human health is therefore one of the criteria for determining the damage to land that can be repaired under the regime laid down by the directive.

From all this it is possible to conclude that for the directive, not all the damages repaired are really those caused to the environment.

<u>2° The cases of authorized or indifferent damages</u>

The directive returns to environmental liability understood in a strict sense: the liability regime does not extend to damage caused to persons and things by the environment. It thus breaks with the solution advocated in the Green Paper, which included in a very broad manner the damage to be repaired[92] .

The directive takes into account the pollution linked to the activities of National Defense, to the consequences of armed conflicts and civil wars. It considers them as outside any repair.

It also excluded from any compensation damage caused by force majeure[93] , removing any uncertainty on the subject, unlike the regime laid down by the Green Paper, which was not clear.

Thus, there are certain permitted damages.

For example, any damage to biodiversity resulting from the act of an operator expressly authorized by article 6, paragraphs 3 and 4, of the "habitats" directive derogates from the principle. For water damage, some damage is justified by "sustainable human development activities"[94] .

---

90 This measure of water damage is the result of the interpretation of Mrs. Pascale Steichen, who also states that the question requires clarification. Pascale Steichen, La proposition de directive du Parlement européen et du Conseil sur la responsabilité environnementale en vue de la prévention et de la réparation des dommages environnementaux, RJ.E février 2003 préc. p.187.
91 Sections 2-18 and 11.
92 See supra, Title 1, Chapter 2, Section 2, B.
93 For example, Article 8 of Directive 2004/35 accepts as a cause for exoneration from liability the act of a third party.
94 Article 4(7) of the Water Directive 2000/60/EC.

§ 2 The determination of the person in charge

<u>A.</u>   <u>The concept of operator</u>

The environmental damages against which the reparation measures will have to intervene are damages caused by professional activities, of private or public law.

The directive states: "Any natural or legal person, private or public, who exercises or controls a professional activity or, where provided for by national legislation, has been delegated significant economic power over the technical operation of the activity, including the holder of a permit or authorisation for such authority, or the person registering or notifying such activity"[95] .

It doesn't matter if these activities are lucrative or not.

The white paper, published in 2000[96] , had recommended the "ultimate recourse" to the liability of parent companies and their managers or of the polluting subsidiary. Thus, in case of insolvency of the subsidiary, or its disappearance, it would have been possible to turn to other potential payers.

The rapporteur for the draft Directive even expressed the wish that the notion of operator be extended to majority shareholders[97] . The system would have been strangely similar to the American C.E.R.C.L.A. law. However, it has been seen that this broad acceptance of the term "responsible person" is very detrimental to legal certainty[98] . Moreover, the Commission has not retained this solution, in order to respect the general rules of corporate law.

This acceptance by the directive of a person in charge has one drawback. As Jean-Pierre Delvigne points out[99] , this definition is too imprecise to avoid difficulties of interpretation. For example, it may allow the search for responsible parties to go well beyond the direct decision-makers. For example, although shareholder liability has not been expressly retained, the idea that any person exercising *"control"* over a business activity can be held liable may lead to the acceptance of liability of majority shareholders. It would have been better to replace the term "control" with "operational management" or "effective", which is a stricter concept.

---

95 Directive n° 2004-35 of April 21, 2004.
96 White Paper on Environmental Liability, COM (2000) 66 final.
97 See the draft opinion of the rapporteur of the European Parliament's Environment Committee of 16 October 2002.
98 See supra, Title I, Chapter 1, Sections 2 and 3.
99 Jean-Pierre Delvigne, La directive sur la responsabilité environnementale, une application du principe pollueur-payeur, Droit de l'Environnement n° 121, September 2004, spec. p.161.

This idea had already appeared in the 2000 White Paper. It is a real feature of the directive.

The principle is that hazardous activities are subject to no-fault liability; non-hazardous activities are subject to fault liability.

Dangerous activities are those defined as such in Annex III of the directive. In fact, this annex refers to the different community regulations for the protection of the environment: the installations subject to the directive of September 24, 1996[100] , concerning the integrated prevention and reduction of pollution, known as "I.P.P.C."[101] , and those relating to the management of waste, water pollution, substances and preparations considered as such, including GMOs.

Operators of other professional activities are favored in two ways. Firstly, they can only be held liable for pollution of the biosphere, and not of water and soil, which is a significant advantage.

On the other hand, they can only be held liable in cases of fault or negligence. This regime is a great step backwards (or a great legal leap forward) towards a more secure liability system for operators.

It should also be noted that the burden of proof of fault lies with the plaintiff. It is not primarily the operator's responsibility to prove that there was no fault.

§ 3 **The causal link**

The causal link is the most essential element of a liability regime. Much abused in the Green Paper and in the Superfund law, it is enshrined in the 2004 Directive[102] . A real causal link must be established by the competent authority in order to engage the liability of an operator, and no presumption of causality such as the "nature of the activity"[103] likely to cause damage or the fact of being on the site of the pollution can be accepted.

The directive also abandoned the idea of joint and several liability (and the distortions of the causal link that would have resulted) for cases of damage caused by the actions or omissions of several operators. It does not, however, permit harmonization, since it leaves the possibility for States to opt for joint and several liability.

---

100 Directive n°96/61 of September 24, 1996, annex I.
101 J.O.C.E., n° L.257 of October 10, 1996.
102 Jean-Pierre Delvigne, La directive sur la responsabilité environnementale : une application du principe pollueur-payeur, Droit de l'environnement, n°121, September 2004, spec.p.163.
103 Article 10 of the draft Convention, supra.

§ 4 The liability action

The solution chosen by the directive aims to prevent the multiplication of actions that would prevent more than it would promote the protection of the environment.

No victim or environmental organization will have a right of action against the operator of the activity causing environmental damage under the 2004 directive.

An action can only be initiated if the above-mentioned persons submit a "request for action" to the competent authority designated by the Member State[104] . This request for action must be accompanied by information and data which will be proof of the reality of the imminence of the damage or its effectiveness[105] .

As a result of this action, the operator must be given the opportunity to explain its position before the authority to which the action is directed decides whether to act. The claimant will have recourse to the courts or to an independent and impartial body.

This acceptance of third parties to act is rather surprising for a system that claims to be one of environmental responsibility. At the same time, it is true that there are no other systems to contain the influx of applications from associations with the same purpose.

§ 5 The repair

One of the major problems of environmental liability is that of reparation and its modalities. Must the sums awarded be used to repair the environment, and if so, what to repair?

The C.E.R.C.L.A. Act had led to allocations of money that had remained unused[106] .

The green paper opted for the obligation to use the money for the rehabilitation of the polluted site, but without giving precise rules on the extent of the repairs.

The directive breaks with these pitfalls and establishes a real system. It provides for two kinds of reparations, a primary one and a "compensatory" one.

Primary repair is any action, including natural regeneration of the natural environment, by which degraded resources or services return to their original state. This can occur without human intervention, or it can be accelerated by artificial means.

Compensatory reparation is reparation "undertaken in respect of resources or services at

---

104 Patrick Thieffry, the directive on environmental liability finally adopted, LPA 21 May 2004, n°102, speculative p. 6.
105 Jean-Pierre Delvigne, *op. cit.* spec. p.161.
106 Patrick Thieffry, L'opportunité d'une responsabilité communautaire du pollueur-payeur entre les Etats-membres et les enseignements de l'expérience américaine, RIDC 1994, p. 103. The site in question could not be rehabilitated, and the sums were too large to be useful.

different locations, as well as any action undertaken to compensate for intermediate losses of natural resources and services that occur between the date of the damage and the primary reparation"[107] .

Damage to water and the biosphere will be repaired by restoring the environment to its original state, which can be done by primary repair and, if necessary, compensatory repair if the primary repair fails to achieve the original state of the site.

Remediation of damage to soils and subsoils should aim to contain, remove or reduce contaminants so as to eliminate any negative impact on human health[108] .

The system of reparation provided for by the directive is more elaborate than that of the Green Paper. The Commission has undoubtedly followed the demands of the industrialists who asked for a strict legal approach to this reparation, notably for questions of financial predictability[109] .

This reference to human health is not surprising given that it is also used as a criterion in the declaration of soil and subsoil pollution. It is logical that the reparation should focus on what allowed the damage to be defined.

Section 3: The Critics

§1 Positive criticism

The system instituted by the directive is more secure than that of the Green Paper. The system is more legal than financial, more respectful of the principles of liability: causal link, exclusion of presumptions such as the "nature of the activity likely to cause damage to the environment".

In addition, the directive incorporates elements of a liability regime that the Green Paper had omitted, and which made the system unsafe for companies, such as the modalities of reparation, the domain of the directive.

Finally, the regime is more of an environmental liability regime than a pollution remediation regime.

---

107 Pascale Steichen, La proposition de directive du Parlement européen et du conseil sur la responsabilité environnementale en vue de la prévention et de la réparation des dommages environnementaux, RJ.E, February 2003, spec. p.190.
108 Patrick Thieffry, La directive sur la responsabilité environnementale enfin adoptée, LPA, 21 Mai 2004, n°102, p.7.
109 The objectives of primary and compensatory repairs have been specified and added to Annex II of the directive, at the request of the industry. Thus, this annex determines the scheme that should guide the choices in terms of repair. It also creates a hierarchy of compensatory remedies, and the competent authorities will decide which ones will be implemented, based on various criteria, including the consequences of the possible measures on public health and safety and the cost of the measures.

§2 Negative criticism

However, several negative criticisms can be made of the directive, particularly in its definition of damage.

First of all, damage to humans is not taken into account at all by the directive, which has taken the opposite path to the Green Paper on this subject. This choice has the great advantage of refocusing reparations on the environment alone, and of better respecting the objective of the directive. The White Paper had moreover proposed on this subject that damage to human health be included in the field of compensation in the case of pollution caused by dangerous activities. The directive did not retain this solution.

Is it therefore coherent to determine the extent of damage to the soil in terms of health while at the same time the damage to this same health will not be repaired?

On the other hand, after analysis of the different types of damages covered by the liability regime of the directive, it appears that not all damages to the environment are covered by the directive. However, the directive was distinguished from other European texts by its desire to create a general regime allowing the repair of all damages caused to the environment by all types of causes or activities.

Is it still a true general environmental responsibility if so much damage caused to the environment is not taken into account by the regime? One may doubt it.

Finally, the directive has taken up the principle of liability for fault, after having established that a system of objective liability is dangerous.

But the concept of fault is only retained for activities not listed in the directive of September 24, 1996[110] , concerning integrated pollution prevention and control, and those relating to waste management, water pollution, and substances and preparations deemed as such.

What justifies such a dichotomy? It is undoubtedly motivated by the need to oblige operators of hazardous activities to be more careful in preventing pollution caused by their activities. But legally the idea is not very satisfactory, because it is too arbitrary.

Environmental protection has evolved rapidly in recent years, thanks in part to changing attitudes.

The directive could have been more inspired by other legislations, which would have allowed it to be in harmony with all the texts on environmental protection.

---

110 Directive n°96/61 of September 24, 1996, annex I.

Chapter 2: Possible improvements

In view of the shortcomings of the provisions of the Directive of April 21, 2004, it seems reasonable to look at other legal rules that show what is missing from the legal regime established by the Directive and that could effectively complement it.

The two developments that can be observed in these texts are a great return to the notion of fault, which is taking on an ever greater role in determining liability (section 1), and the emergence of the use of contractual relations in environmental liability, a point completely forgotten by the directive (section 2).

The first evolution is found in the "Reach" project, which influences environmental liability law.

Section 1 The Reach project and the growing role of fault

The proposal of the European Commission called "Reach"[111] was brought before the European Parliament by the European Commission in October 2003 and adopted in first reading on November 17, 2005. On December 13, the Council of Ministers reached an agreement, which would allow its entry into force in early 2007.

A brief overview of the system in place is necessary to appreciate the potential liability implications of the proposal.

§ 1 The settlement plan

The proposal establishes information requirements based on the precautionary principle.

It imposes on producers a new obligation to register chemical substances[112] . The purpose of this obligation is to ensure better sharing of data by producers on the risks discovered for these substances. This means that producers will not only have to communicate the physico-chemical properties and the harmful consequences on health and the environment of these products to users, but will also have to request their registration and authorization by the European Chemicals Control Agency[113] .

In addition, users will have to communicate to their suppliers the inconveniences they may have noticed when using the products. This communication will have to be done either

---

111 Reach: acronym that comes from : Registration, Evaluation, Authorization of Chemicals. The rapporteur responsible for this proposal was the European deputy Guido Sacconi, the proposal was adopted by 398 votes against 148. " L'environnement pour les européens ", n°22, January 2006, p.7.
112 Arnaud Gossement, l'incidence du projet Reach sur la responsabilité du producteur de produits chimiques, Gaz. Pal. Rec. nov.-dec. 2005, doctrine p.3851
113 Arnaud Gossement, *op.cit.*

directly between registrants or through the Agency.

The third category of recipients of this information is of course employers, workers and consumers. They will have to be able to access all the information relating to the risks of the products supplied. This measure was taken as a consequence of the asbestos affair, where companies had been reproached for not having put in place any of the information measures provided for by the regulations (job description, exposure sheet, etc.).

In the absence of this information, producers and users will be held liable for failure to comply with very specific information obligations, obligations that are necessary for the application of the precautionary principle. It is therefore a notion of fault that is used in the proposal.

However, it must be stressed that the proposal does not provide for a specific liability regime in the event of breaches of the information obligations, i.e. in the event of damage resulting from the breach of these obligations. Such a regime should be provided for.

Liability for fault would thus be general to all chemicals new since 1981, without exception according to their dangerousness. On the other hand, it must be emphasized that this system is more favorable than a traditional liability system, since the burden of proof no longer lies with the victim but with the presumed perpetrator of the damage. This is what emerges from the Reach proposal.

§ 2 The value of the regulation

A.   The overlap with the directive

Unlike Directive 2004/35, the Reach project focuses exclusively on the establishment of a single and coherent Community system on "chemicals". The proposal not only sets up a system of responsibility in the repair of damage caused to the environment by its products, it also tackles the prevention by an original system, the information between companies on the various chemicals found on the market.

The text of Article 1er sums up its purpose quite well: "This Regulation is based on the principle that manufacturers, importers and downstream users have a responsibility to ensure that they manufacture, place on the market, import or use substances that are not likely to have harmful effects on human health or the environment. Its provisions are based on the precautionary principle.

The proposal therefore does not really address the same issues as the directive. This article 1er highlights that the proposal completely links harm to human health with harm to the environment, whereas the directive only takes into account harm to health in the specific case of polluted soil.

On the other hand, the proposal targets only chemicals, and thus considerably restricts its field of application, since in all cases of environmental damage other than by chemicals, the REACH system cannot be used. The directive does not focus on a specific cause of environmental damage.

However, in practice, most of the damage to the environment is caused by chemicals. For example, pollution by industries, agricultural products such as fertilizers and pesticides are the most encountered pollution of rivers and soils, if only by the amount of products used in these economic sectors. And the damage caused to the biosphere is mainly through chemicals.

Contrary to appearances, the field of the Reach system is therefore largely the same as the field of the 2004 directive, and the liability regime resulting from this proposal could duplicate the directive in these areas of environmental damage.

Indeed, in the event of environmental damage caused by a company due to the leakage of chemical products, for example, if there has been a violation of the information obligations, the parties wishing to obtain compensation from the polluter may rely on both the REACH regulation and the directive of 21 April 2004. In one case, the liability will be based on the violation of the prevention obligation. In the other case, liability will depend on whether the activity is dangerous or not, and on the recognition of a fault.

The Reach proposal has wider consequences than what is merely provided for in these recitals: it demonstrates a return to fault in European liability law.

B.   The return of fault in environmental liability law

The disrespect of the precautionary principle gives rise to a new fault, which is what emerges from a French doctrinal debate that began after the vote of the law of February 2, 1995 on the reinforcement of the protection of the environment[114] . The question raised was to know whether the action in a situation of scientific uncertainty made it possible to engage the liability of the author of the damage on the basis of risk or on the basis of fault.

Some authors prefer the notion of liability for risk. For it seems that this objective liability has the advantage of being well adapted to any fault committed in the scientific environment, especially when scientific uncertainty is involved. Proof of fault may be

---

114 Cf. Gilles Martin, la mise en œuvre du principe de précaution et la renaissance de la responsabilité pour faute, JCP éd. Suppl. Cahiers du droit de l'entreprise, 15 April 1999, p.3.

difficult, if not impossible, to obtain for the victim, for several reasons.

On the one hand, there is often a long delay between the occurrence of the injury and the realization of the damage, which requires an uncertain historical research on the scientific knowledge of the moment of the realization of the risk in order to be able to admit the responsibility of the author of the damage.

On the other hand, the evidence requires scientific skills that are far beyond the capabilities of the parties.

However, strict liability has a defect that it is essential to take into account in the protection of the environment: it does not allow for the search for the origin of the prejudice, and thus the prevention of new prejudice. The purpose of bringing a case before the court is as much to obtain compensation for the damage as it is to avoid further damage for the same facts. Liability for fault leads the parties to search in depth for the origins of the risk, and to eliminate them, which is not the case in the search for objective liability.

This is what would have made the initiators of the Reach system lean towards accepting fault-based liability, rather than strict liability.

According to Mr. Arnaud Gossement[115] , this choice has major consequences for the general liability of companies for environmental pollution: European liability regimes will be less and less reluctant to use fault as a basis for holding polluters liable.

The regimes that will follow the Reach Regulation will certainly take this route.

One may then wonder why the Commission, which wanted to establish a general liability regime (the directive of 21 April 2004), only partially chose fault as the basis of the liability regime. It would have been better if it had followed completely the orientation initiated in this matter, at the risk of finding itself out of step with the rest of environmental liability law.

In addition to fault, the directive could rely on contractual relationships.

Section 2: The Use of Civil Relations in Corporate Liability

§ 1 The value of using contracts

The other means available to the States and the Union to prevent and sanction any environmental damage is the use of civil society, as shown by the Aarhus Convention in its part on access to information[116] .

---

115 Cf. in particular: Arnaud Gossement, l'incidence du projet Reach sur la responsabilité du producteur de produits chimiques, Gaz. Pal. Rec. nov.-dec. 2005, doctrine p.3851.
116 United Nations Convention, June 23-25, 1998, on access to information, public participation in decision-

According to this convention, the pursuit of their private interests by the parties to a contract allows the protection of the general interest. It is the solution already chosen by certain legal systems to give a place to the civil contract as a means of protecting the environment. The European institutions could draw inspiration from this to perfect the current system of civil liability.

This recourse to civil law can be explained by the development of the idea according to which environmental protection should not be thought of in isolation, but in relation to economic perspectives, perspectives of sustainable development. The need to put in place strategies that combine economic growth with the maintenance of ecosystems is better understood today[117] , and to do this, property and more generally private rights would allow for good management of natural resources. Thus, the only way to properly protect the environment would no longer be the intervention of the State, the preferred solution today[118] , but the use of private relations.

This environmental protection is manifested in two ways.

First, many economic agents are more concerned about protecting the environment today than they were fifteen years ago, and this is reflected in contracts. This is the result of the evolution of mentalities in society and if this change in the mentalities of contracting parties is not absolute, it is nevertheless sufficiently present to be taken into account legally[119] .

Secondly, and most importantly, it would be possible through appropriate legislation to make the parties to a contract commit to environmental protection through the obligation to insert special clauses. For although the ethical willingness of companies has increased in recent years, this is certainly not sufficient for the proper protection of the environment, and it is obvious that mandatory measures are necessary.

In this respect, the obligation to inform clause seems particularly well adapted to environmental protection.

By this clause, a contractor would be obliged to inform his co-contractor of the present or future environmental damage on the site in question.

---

making and access to justice in environmental matters. Ratified by France by law n° 2002-285 of February 28, 2002.

117 O. Godard, Environnement et économie : l'inscription économique du développement durable, in Enjeux et politiques de l'environnement, Cahiers français n°306, janvier-février 2002, Doc. Fr.p.52.

118 G. Parléani, Marché et environnement, Droit env. mars 2005, p.52.

119 We can cite examples of banks that require their co-contractors to respect environmental standards. Thus, a French bank in 2006 offers a subsidized loan for any project with an ecological character and in line with an environmental approach. Other banks have set up environmental questionnaires before granting loans. Still others oblige companies to submit to the European ELMAS regulation which allows voluntary companies to undergo an environmental audit.

Thus, it has the advantage of facilitating the discovery of polluted sites, and their timely remediation, because often the problem with site pollution is that it has remained hidden for too long; the damage has then had time to worsen.

Second, it facilitates the history of successive activities on the site in question. Each party notifying the other of the risky activities carried out on the site, the chain of information is not easily broken.

Finally, it would be a private means of controlling the risks associated with a polluting activity. Indeed, in order to fulfill its information obligation, each party will have environmental audits carried out, and the risks and damages caused to the environment will not remain ignored.

Companies will control all the better if they know that their responsibility can be called into question on the basis of these information clauses, and that they could then be led to repair the damage caused by their co-contractors[120].

In order to protect the environment by making it easier to hold the contracting parties liable, the French legislator has already used contracts. The legislator has taken up the principle of protection of the environment through private clauses by obliging the parties to fulfil information obligations. This obligation is therefore no longer entirely a matter of autonomy of will, but also serves the general interest[121].

§ 2 The French example

Several examples of domestic law allow us to understand this recourse to private relationships made by the legislator in our law.

The Environmental Code gives a number of them.

First of all, art. L.514-20 of this code, which concerns the case of the sale of a site on which an activity subject to authorization has been carried out. With this text, the legislator obliges the seller to declare all the past activities carried out on this site, and the significant risks and inconveniences that may have resulted from them[122]. What is very interesting in

---

120 This control would undoubtedly be supplemented by a control by the insurance companies, which can, on the spot, check the veracity of the information communicated. This power of insurance is reflected in the contracts, which provide for the insurer's power to visit the sites operated and to verify the conditions under which the insured carries out its activities. This multiplication of controls by people with financial interests at stake is excellent for the protection of the environment. See Assurpol contracts, *in* Lamy environnement installations classées, 840-5.

121 Jérôme Attard, Contrats et environnement : quand l'obligation d'information devient instrument de développement durable, LPA, 26 January 2006, p.7, spec. paragraph 5.

122 W. Grandpré, L'obligation d'information du vendeur d'un terrain dans la loi sur les installations classées, Dr. Env. January-February 2000, p.15.

this text is that this obligation is not only incumbent on the operator of an activity, or the owner of the building at the time of the polluting activity, but on any seller of a site on which a dangerous activity may have been carried out at one time. This obliges the seller to carry out historical research on the site.

It is therefore a real "duty to remember" the risks that this article creates.

This obligation is also found in art. L.125-5 of the Environment Code[123] . The seller or lessor of a property must inform the purchaser or lessee of a property located in a zone covered by a "technological risk prevention plan" of its situation, and of the existence of losses that would have given rise to insurance compensation, or of which he or she would have been aware when he or she purchased the property. Here again, the duty to inform is in line with the principle of researching the history of the site, and the person must communicate the information that he or she has had or could have obtained.

Finally, art. 541-23 of the Environmental Code makes anyone who has handed over, or caused to be handed over, this type of waste to someone other than the operator of an approved disposal facility jointly and severally liable.

All these examples show that it is conceivable to use contractual relations to constitute a liability regime for environmental damage.

§ 3 The lack of consideration of civil relations in European environmental liability law

The directive establishes a liability regime that does not give much room to private parties[124] . Thus, no private party can bring an action before the courts to obtain the liability of a polluter. It is the public authority that is responsible for this.

Similarly, reparable damages are defined by the regulations.

The directive would have benefited greatly from defining a less public law based more on the interests of the parties. In particular, it could have followed the French example, which bases its government policy on contractual relations[125] .

This solution is the one that France, but also several other European countries, seems to

---

123 Established by law n° 2003-699 of July 30, 2003 on "the prevention of technological and natural risks and the repair of damages".

124 Isabelle Doussan, Le droit de la responsabilité civile française à l'épreuve de la " responsabilité environnementale " instaurée par la directive du 21 avril 2004, LPA, p.3. She even qualifies the directive as "an appendix to preventive regulations", as a "mechanism complementary to the powers of the administration", considering that the directive cannot be considered as instituting a liability regime.

125 Jérôme Attard, Contrats et environnement : quand l'obligation d'information devient instrument de développement durable, LPA, 26 January 2006, p.9.

be moving towards, and it is all the more surprising that the 2004 directive was silent on this solution. It was apparently one of its objectives to harmonize European legislation; in this case, it would have been desirable for it to be inspired by the legislation of European countries in all of the solutions that they put in place. Especially since this solution seems to be the future of environmental liability.

****

In the 1990s, with the discovery of the multiple risks to humans from industrial pollution, legal systems turned to no-fault liability, which seemed the most likely to protect the environment and allow its restoration.

Faced with the significant imperfections of this type of regime, the European Union returned to a more traditional fault-based liability regime. However, it did not go to the end of its reasoning, applying fault only to a part of professional activities, those considered dangerous.

While the regime it establishes with the 2004 directive is more respectful of the legal principles of a liability regime, it does not really follow the general evolution observed for environmental liability.

The Union could have gone further.

By limiting the application of the regime of the directive to certain damages, by limiting the use of fault, by involving the State to the detriment of private parties and contractual relations, the Commission has diminished the interest of the directive for the future.

However, by identifying ecological damage and determining the extent and scope of compensation, this 2004 directive, although imperfect, has the merit of laying the foundations of a future European regime.

BIBLIOGRAPHY

Works

Michel **Prieur**, "Droit de l'Environnement", Dalloz, 4e edition, p. 404

Special Reviews

Monographies sur l'environnement, n° 42, *L'assurance pollution*, 1992, p.7

The environment for Europeans, n°22, January 2006, p.7

Jurisclasseur International, Civil Liability

Lamy environnement installations classées, 840-5

Articles

Jérôme **Attard**, Contrats et environnement : quand l'obligation d'information devient instrument de développement durable, LPA, 26 January 2006, p. 3

M. **Bocken**, "la réparation des dommages causés par la pollution en droit belge", R.G.D.C., 1992, p. 284.

Andrée **Brunet**, La régulation juridique des questions environnementales et le principe de subsidiarité, Gaz. Pal. Vend. 11, Sat. 12 June 2004, p. 1705

Jean-Pierre **Delvigne**, La directive sur la responsabilité environnementale, une application du principe pollueur-payeur, Droit de l'Environnement n° 121, September 2004, spec. p.161

Isabelle **Doussan**, The French law of civil liability in the test of the

"Environmental liability" introduced by the directive of 21 April 2004, LPA, 25 August 2005, p.3

O. **Godard**, Environnement et économie : l'inscription économique du développement durable, in Enjeux et politiques de l'environnement, Cahiers français n°306, janvier-février 2002, Doc. Fr.p.52

Arnaud **Gossement**, l'incidence du projet Reach sur la responsabilité du producteur de produits chimiques, Gaz. Pal. Rec. nov.-dec. 2005, doctrine p.3851

W. **Grandpré**, L'obligation d'information du vendeur d'un terrain dans la loi sur les installations classées, Dr. Env. janvier-février 2000, p.15

H.W. **Hoffman**, La responsabilité civile pollution et son assurance en Allemagne, RGAT,

1992.474

Christian **Huglo**, "Towards the recognition of a right of nature to reparation", Petites Affiches, September 29, 1993, n° 117, p. 15

G. **Husson**, le point de vue des assureurs, *in Le dommage écologique en droit interne, communautaire et comparé,* Economica, 1992, p. 179

Barbara **Jesus-Gimeno**, Protection of the environment through criminal law, for a community approach, Environment, May 2002, p.8

Christian **Larroumet**, La responsabilité civile en matière d'environnement. Le projet de Convention du Conseil de l'Europe et le livre vert de la Commission des Communautés européennes, Dalloz 1994, chron. p.101

P.A.L. **Machado**, Les sanctions pénales en matière d'environnement, *in* Réunion mondiale des associations de droit de l'environnement, déclaration de Limoges, 16 novembre 1990, préc.p.16

Gilles **Martin**, la mise en œuvre du principe de précaution et la renaissance de la responsabilité pour faute, JCP éd. Suppl. Cahiers du droit de l'entreprise, 15 April 1999, p.3

G. **Parléani**, Marché et environnement, Droit env. mars 2005, p.52

Michel **Prieur**, L'environnement entre dans la Constitution, LPA, n° 134, 7 July 2005, p.14

H. **Smets**, le principe pollueur-payeur, un principe économique érigé en principe de droit de l'environnement, RGDI *publ.* 1993.339

Patricia **Savin**, Le droit à l'environnement, Gaz. Pal. Vend.17, Sat.18 March 2006, p. 52

Vincent **Sol** - Un droit en pleine évolution, LPA, 8 August 2000, n°157, p. 18

-       Sanctions and responsibilities in environmental law: the American experience, RDAI, n°7, 1993, p.869

Pascale **Steichen**, La proposition de directive du Parlement européen et du conseil sur la responsabilité environnementale en vue de la prévention et de la réparation des dommages environnementaux, RJ.E, February 2003, p.177

Patrick **Thieffry** - L'opportunité d'une responsabilité communautaire du pollueur ; Les distorsions entre les Etats-membres et les enseignements de l'expérience américaine, RIDC, 1994, 1-1994,p.103

\-	Corporate environmental responsibility, the European projects are becoming clearer, LPA of February 21, 2003, p.4

\-	The directive on environmental liability finally adopted, LPA, 21 May 2004, n°102, p.5

\-	The reinforcement of the environmental responsibility of companies: divergent French and European trends, Gaz. Pal. May-June 2004, p.1717

Geneviève **Viney**, Les principaux aspects de la responsabilité civile des entreprises pour atteinte à l'environnement en droit français, JCP 1996, I.3900

Official documents

Directive n° 79/409 of April 2, 1979, O.J.C.E. n°L 103 of April 29, 1979

Directive 85/374 EEC of 25 July 1985

Directive No. 92/43 of the European Parliament and of the Council of 21 May 1992, OJEC, No. L.206, 22 July 1992

Directive n°96/61 of 24 September 1996, OJEC, n° L.257 of 10 October 1996

Directive 2000/60 of 23 October 2000, OJEC No. L 237 of 22 December 2000

Directive n° 2004/35 of April 21, 2004

Regulation 309/94 of 15 December 1994, OJEC n° L.333 22 December 1994

The draft opinion of the rapporteur of the European Parliament's Committee on the Environment of 16 October 2002

White Paper on Environmental Liability, COM (2000)

German Environmental Liability Act of 10 December 1990, Bundesgesetzblatt, Part I, No. 67 of 14 December 1990, p. 2634

Belgian law of 22 July 1974

Greek Law No. 1650 of 1986, Article 29

French law n°92-1444 of December 31, 1992 (D. and ALD. 1993.106)

French law n°90-1130 of December 19, 1990

Decree n°89-648 of August 31, 1989

Web sites

psychobiology.ouvaton.org/glossary/txt-p06.20-04-glossary.htm

http://eduscol.education.fr/D0185/concepts.htm

buongiornoeuropa.istruzione.it/glossario/en/lettera e en.shtml

www.europa.eu.int/comm/environment/chemicals/reach.htm

Printed by Books on Demand GmbH, Norderstedt / Germany